Cindy, Darla & I
found this book in the
UK, & so much enjoyed
reading it together.

My Friends
who don't have
Dogs

Read & share with Jessie.

Love

KfD

My Friends who don't have Dogs

Anna Levin

For JB, remembering Tobermory days
with Mulligan and Tag, my four-legged
flatmates who taught me so much.

Special thanks to Jessica, for
encouragement and Canna

First published in Great Britain by Merlin Unwin Books Ltd 2021

Merlin Unwin Books Ltd
Palmers House
7 Corve Street
Ludlow
Shropshire SY8 1DB

www.merlinunwin.co.uk

ISBN 978-1-913159-33-7

Designed by Simon Bishop
Typeset in Magdelin and Good Silent Night
Cover illustration by Mary Collett @linoprints
Printed by IMAK

*O*nce upon a time I was in a right old grump about the housework and the disproportionate contribution our four-legged family member makes to the general grime. I wondered briefly why we share our homes and lives with these mucky creatures. Then I remembered. This is for all my friends who do have dogs...

My friends
who don't have dogs
don't have...

Permanent snow drifts of dirty old hair
in every corner and skirting board
and every tread of every stair

And soggy dog splatters
up the walls of the hall

And muddy paws
on newly-washed floors

Or the hoover clogged
with the usual mix
of bits of bones
and chewed-up sticks.

My friends who don't have dogs
don't hold conversations with their
neighbours and friends

While holding little black plastic bags
as discreetly as possible
and yet at arm's length

They don't have to think
of things they'd rather do
on dark, rainy mornings
than picking up poo.

My friends who don't have dogs
don't know the humiliation and shame
when you're calling, pleading, scolding, begging
SHOUTING out a name

To no avail, it's all in vain,
you're left foolish and bereft
because your dear companion,
your most loyal friend, is momentarily deaf

And bolts for the horizon
and there's nothing you can do
because that squirrel, that bird, that scent,
is just more interesting than you.

My friends who don't have dogs
don't have awkward silences
with their overnight guests

Fretting over breakfast
about which moment might be best to
break the awful news...

... that their shoes
have been
chewed.

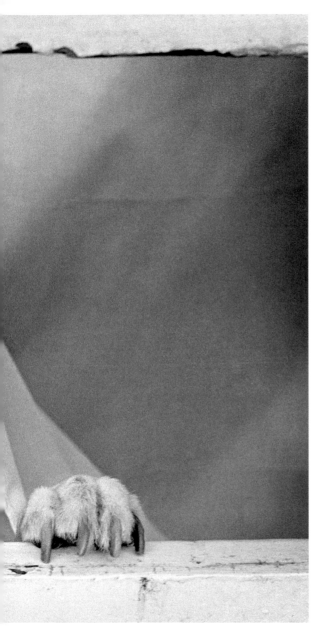

But then...

My friends who don't have dogs don't have
a personal trainer on their case
each and every day

Who says: come on, don't cower
from wind and weather

Come on, grab your wellies,
we'll face it together.

Come on! Come on!
Let's go! Come on!

We've got to get outside!

Till we're windswept
and weather-worn
wet and muddy
and bramble-torn

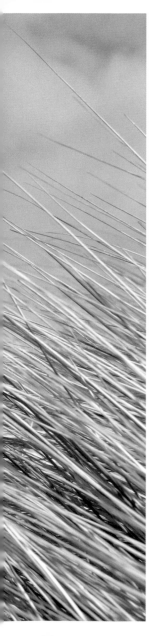

and suddenly... alive!

My friends who don't have dogs
sometimes say

That they would,
well, they might,
quite like a dog

Maybe
one day

But not yet; they want their freedom
and their holidays.

I tell them freedom's
what my dog gives
not what he takes away

Freedom to feel
the deep green hush
of the open fields
and the woods at dusk

Freedom from fear
to walk into the night
my own sweet bodyguard
at my side

Freedom to set aside
chores and cares
and throw sticks and seaweed
into the air

A little pool of freedom
in the clamour of each day

When we take the time to play.

And they don't have a philosopher
all of their own
to guide and remind them
from the comfort of their home

With wise brown eyes
that neither know nor care

About wealth or status
or clothes or hair

A life coach
with daily reminders
that the best things in life
are free

Who says:
you want to
reach high?
Climb a mountain

Do you want to be rich,
rich like me?

Come, we'll run across miles of golden sand
and we'll splash in the silvery sea.

And they don't have
a waste disposal unit
poised to ensure
that no crumbs
hit the floor

And they don't get an ecstatic welcome
each time they come in the front door

From a sweet-faced, beloved companion
who just wants to be near

And who asks for nothing more than a play...

... and a sleep

...and a feed

... and maybe a scratch,
right there, behind the ear.

My friends who don't have dogs
don't see
the place of a dog in the heart of a home
how they're part of the family

And the bonds that form
and grow through time,
as we live together, lives entwined

And the scale of the loss
that's left behind
when it's time to say goodbye.

And they don't know
how good it feels
to bury your head in the scent
of warm neck and breathe

And if you're hurting, or hating
or feeling alone
or aching, or weary
or far from home

There is absolute comfort
in a single touch
of cold, wet nose
against your hand

Something my friends
who don't have dogs
may never understand.

Credits

Page	Dog	Photographer
2	Layla	Dan Jolley
5	(Footprints)	Bas Fürst
6	Savannah	Gill Crane*
9	Luna	Lauren Werrell
11	Milo	Abigail Evans
12	Maurice	Gaby Harrison
14	Indie	Zoe Colville
16	Billy	Ida Maspero
18	Sherlock	Laurie Campbell
20	Coco	Victoria Galbraith
23	Layla	Dan Jolley*
24	Unknown	Bj Stewart
26	Bramble	Laurie Campbell
29	Unknown	Bj Stewart
30	Rummy	Maria Pound
32	Floyd	Bj Stewart
35	Gucchi	Bj Stewart
37	Ellie	Paige Ingram
38	Cyder	Bj Stewart
41	Craig	Bj Stewart
42	Pip	Dan Jolley
44	Mabel	Berry Smith
46	Shiloh	Berry Smith
49	Sinah	Ellen Kempers and Maarten Meijer
50	Ruby	Rob Outram
53	Meg & Ruby	Rachel Court
54	Bella	Harriet Collett
56	Cuillin	Julie Ogilvie
58	Chewy	Roderick MacKenzie
61	Spot	Bj Stewart
62	Ruby	Rob Outram
64	Freddie	Sue Bradley
67	Lucy	Elizabeth Nicholson
68	Sinah	Ellen Kempers
70	Sinah	Maarten Meijer
73	Jed	Wanda Sowry
74	Charlie and Bess	Joanne Potter
76	Gizmo	Julie Mezzone
77	Cyder	Bj Stewart
78	Frankie	Andreas Kelch
81	Beau	Laurie Campbell
82	Fionnbharr	Jay Butler
83	Dexter	Hannah Miles
86	Tilly	Gina Finch
89	Jess	Louisa Mann
90	Sinah	Ellen Kempers and Maarten Meijer
93	Billy	Ida Maspero
94	Tara	Maeve Bishop
97	Ruby, Dill, Monty, Ella and Martha	Christina Cheong
99	Chango Mutney	Fran Levin
101	Max	Joanne Potter
102	Pip	Dan Jolley
104	Savannah	Gill Crane
106	Maurice	Gaby Harrison
108	Jasper	Sharon Dewstowe
111	Cyder	Bj Stewart
112	Rhaegar	Emmie Parton
113	Rusty	Bj Stewart
115	Roy, Beauty and Benjamin	Bj Stewart
116	Jamie	Bj Stewart
118	Bella	Harriet Collett
120	Dennis	Julian Taylor
122	Budweiser	Jo Evans
124	Sherlock and Hugo	Laurie Campbell
126	Maurice	Gaby Harrison
128	Unknown	Laurie Campbell

* SOS Podenco Rescue: www.sospodencorescue.com